Access your online resources

Supporting Children with DLD is accompanied by a number of printable online materials, designed to ensure this resource best supports your professional needs.

Activate your online resources:

Go to www.routledge.com/cw/speechmark and click on the cover of this book.

Click the 'Sign in or Request Access' button and follow the instructions in order to access the resources.

Supporting Children with DLD

Supporting Children with DLD has been developed to help raise awareness of Developmental Language Disorder, and to highlight the impact of the condition from the child's point of view.

With activities, prompts and sample questions, this is an essential resource to enable adults to understand the reality of living with DLD, helping children feel heard and respected, as well as providing a solid foundation for tailoring support to individual needs. Drawing on specific examples from *Harry's Story*, the book does not assume any prior knowledge of DLD and is designed to offer the reader accessible information and practical advice, teaching as you go.

This book:

- Highlights the link between spoken and written language, addressing the need to recognise the literary difficulties faced by children with DLD
- Provides practical activities and worksheets that can be used to help children express themselves and ask for help
- Offers strategies for supporting children's understanding of language, based on common situations and experiences explored in *Harry's Story*

Written to be an accessible introduction to DLD and its effect on children's lives, this is an essential resource for parents and professionals looking to understand the condition.

Kate Kempton is a community speech and language therapist in Devon, who works with children in early years and school settings. Kate has a particular interest in Developmental Language Disorder and after completing a Masters in Language and Literacy at the University of Sheffield, became increasingly aware of the links between spoken and written language. This led to a further interest in narrative language and the importance of being able to tell and share our stories.

Supporting Children with DLD

A User Guide About Developmental Language Disorder

KATE KEMPTON

Routledge
Taylor & Francis Group

LONDON AND NEW YORK

Cover image: Kate Kempton

First published 2022
by Routledge
4 Park Square, Milton Park, Abingdon, Oxon OX14 4RN

and by Routledge
605 Third Avenue, New York, NY 10158

Routledge is an imprint of the Taylor & Francis Group, an informa business

British Library Cataloguing-in-Publication Data
A catalogue record for this book is available from the British Library

Library of Congress Cataloging-in-Publication Data
A catalog record for this book has been requested

ISBN: 978-1-032-17138-8 (pbk)
ISBN: 978-1-003-25196-5 (ebk)

DOI: 10.4324/9781003251965

Typeset in Antitled
by Apex CoVantage, LLC

Access the companion website: www.routledge.com/cw/speechmark

To Sally, for teaching me the value of every child's experience,
and to see the world from their view.

Contents

Acknowledgements

I would love to say a very big thank you to my wonderful family for your infinite patience and love. Thank you to everyone who read my work, your kind words were such a help. Special thanks to Rose for your continued enthusiasm and for encouraging me to share *Harry's Story*. Thank you to Clare and Leah at Speechmark for your calm support in bringing this project together.

Introduction

The picture book, *Harry's Story*, is primarily intended for children with DLD and was written with this group of children in mind, however, it would also be suitable to share with typically developing children, as part of a wider conversation about our individual strengths and differences.

The story and associated activities would be most suited to children aged between 6 and 11 years, but this may vary according to the individual needs and abilities of each child.

The user guide was developed alongside the picture book, as a support for families and friends, teachers and other professionals who work with this group of children. It aims to provide information about DLD, along with activities, strategies and ideas you can use with your child, to help them talk about their experience of DLD.

The user guide does not assume any prior knowledge of DLD and is designed to offer the reader accessible information and practical advice, teaching you as you go. It is intended to accompany the picture book *Harry's Story* and draws on specific examples from this book.

DOI: 10.4324/9781003251965-1

Considerations

Drawing and pictures

In the story, Harry enjoys drawing and it helps him to express his stories.

Some children with DLD may also like drawing their ideas, rather than writing them down, especially during the creative stages of writing. However, this won't be the same for every child. Many children can feel self-conscious about their drawing, so it is important to let your child choose what helps them best.

If your child does choose to draw, remember to let them tell you what their picture means. Their picture of a tiger might not look like a tiger to you, but if that's what it means to them, it is important to respect this.

If your child doesn't want to draw, perhaps you could help them take some photographs or print out some pictures to represent their ideas. You could even sketch your child's ideas whilst they say them out loud. I have found that children really enjoy watching the pictures emerge and you certainly don't have to be amazing at drawing!

You could then use the photographs or pictures to help your child remember and sequence their stories or ideas.

Talking about DLD

Harry's Story can be used to support conversations with your child about DLD and as a prompt to talk about what's hard for them at school, as well as what helps. These conversations might not always be easy for your child because of the associated language demands. There are some strategies in Chapter 3 to support you and your child with this, however, it might be that they are simply not ready. It is important to respect this. If your child is not ready to talk about their own feelings and experiences just yet, that's fine. They might still enjoy talking about what happens to Harry in the story and this is still a positive starting point.

DOI: 10.4324/9781003251965-2

1. What is DLD?

Developmental Language Disorder, or DLD, is a type of communication disorder, which develops during early childhood and affects children's understanding and use of spoken of language. It has been called different names in the past, including Specific Language Impairment (SLI) but Developmental Language Disorder (DLD) is the new term, agreed by an international panel of experts (Bishop et al., 2016, 2017). It is hoped that by universally and consistently using the term 'DLD', it will help raise awareness of DLD and provide better support to children and adults with this condition.

Facts about DLD

- There is no known cause of DLD, but evidence suggests that biological environmental and genetic risk factors, can influence whether a child develops DLD (Bishop et al., 2017).
- DLD is not caused by another biomedical condition, such as cerebral palsy, a hearing loss, or autism spectrum disorder (Bishop et al., 2017). Children with these conditions generally do experience language difficulties but would be classed as having a language disorder alongside or associated with the other condition.
- DLD develops during the early years, but a diagnosis is rarely given to children under the age of five. Some children are slower to start talking but catch up spontaneously and have typical language skills by the time they start school. Other children, however, have language difficulties that persist beyond the age of five and this might be an indicator of DLD.
- Children with DLD typically experience difficulties with several different language skills, for example: understanding and remembering instructions; learning and remembering new words; understanding sentences; putting words and sentences in the right order; understanding jokes and sarcasm.
- DLD affects different children in different ways and each child's strengths and needs will vary. This means it is essential to treat every child with DLD as an individual and find out how DLD is affecting them specifically.
- DLD is a long-term condition which means that people with DLD are likely to experience some challenges with language throughout their life.

Why do we need to raise awareness of DLD?

- DLD is much more common than you might think and affects just over 7% of children which is around two children in every class of 30 (Norbury et al., 2016).

DOI: 10.4324/9781003251965-3

- If more people learn about DLD it might make it easier for teachers and parents to recognise and understand the needs of these children.
- Children with DLD are often good at masking their language difficulties which means their needs may be missed.
- It is important for children with DLD to be identified earlier and given the specific support they need. When appropriate provision is offered, children with DLD can be helped to achieve their social and academic potential and the impact of their DLD can be reduced (Royal College of Speech and Language Therapists, 2018).
- It is important that teaching staff know about DLD because these children are at greater risk of social and academic difficulties if their needs are not properly supported in the classroom environment (Catts et al., 2002). Children may struggle to keep up with lessons, if they don't understand the words or haven't understood what the teacher has explained to the class.
- It's important for children and young people to know about DLD too. It may help children with DLD understand their needs and why they find some things more difficult. It might also encourage people who don't have DLD, to listen and to be more empathetic to those who do.

What is language and why is it so important?

What is language?

- Language is a complex process involving successful integration of several different skills. It refers to how we understand and use words when they are arranged together in sentences.
- Understanding spoken language is referred to as 'receptive language'. Using spoken language is referred to as 'expressive language'.
- Children with DLD have primary difficulties with spoken language, however, in most cases written language skills will also impacted.
- Children with DLD experience difficulties learning their own language(s). Bilingual children can also have DLD, in which case they would have difficulties learning both or all the languages they are exposed to.

The following section explains the different skills that we need to integrate in order to communicate successfully with language.

Listening and Attention

Listening and attention skills are the foundations that underpin language and communication development. Children need to be able to tune in and focus on spoken language in their environment before they can begin to understand it. Some children have specific difficulties with attention, and may need individual support to develop this skill.

Children with DLD might appear to have difficulties with attention. It might be hard for a child to listen and pay attention if someone is using too many long sentences that they don't understand.

Pragmatics

Pragmatics refers to the social use of language and communication. This includes the ability to understand and use gestures, body language, facial expressions and tone of voice. It also includes turn taking and joining in appropriately with conversation.

Many children with DLD are good at using body language and gestures to support their communication, but they may still experience difficulties with social interactions. This is often associated with the language demands of many social situations. For example, keeping up with the pace of conversation in a group, understanding non-literal language, humour and sarcasm.

Working memory

Working memory refers to the ability to hold information in our memory long enough to process it. This can include verbal information such as sounds, words and sentences.

Children with DLD may struggle to hold and manipulate verbal information in their working memory, especially if there are a lot of unfamiliar words. This means it can be more difficult for children with DLD to learn new words or to remember long and complex instructions.

Vocabulary

Vocabulary refers to the words used in a given language. We use the word 'vocabulary' to describe the words that an individual understands and the words they use in their spoken or written language. Vocabulary is a crucial part of language development and is found to be significantly associated with academic and reading outcomes (Muter et al., 2004).

Reduced vocabulary knowledge and word finding difficulties are a common feature of DLD (Bishop et al., 2017).

Grammar

Grammar refers to the rules and organisation of language and determines how words and sentences are arranged to show meaning.

Most children learn the rules of language without too much difficulty, but children with DLD typically have persisting difficulties understanding and using grammar (Bishop et al., 2017).

Children with DLD might struggle to understand and use more complex sentence structures and might not know, for example, that 'the boy kicked the girl' means something different to 'the boy was kicked by the girl'.

Inference

Inference relates to understanding the overall meaning of language and filling in the gaps when information is not explicitly given. So, for example, in the following sentence: 'Lily loved swimming, she went to Little Dolphins every week', we can infer that 'she' refers to Lily and 'Little Dolphins' is probably the name of her swimming club.

Children with DLD can struggle to infer meaning or read between the lines, because of their already fragile language skills. This means that they can't rely on their language skills for clues in the same way that their peers might. It can also be difficult for children with DLD to keep up with jokes, sarcasm or other social language that rely on 'inference and' 'word-play'.

Narrative

Narrative simply means storytelling and includes both fictional and real-life stories. Children use narrative skills every day to talk about what happened in the playground or what they did at the weekend, which helps them make sense of their experiences and connect with those around them. Children also learn narrative through sharing picture books and stories and spoken narrative ability is found to be positively associated with later literacy outcomes (Pinto, Tarchi, & Bigozzi, 2015; Griffin et al., 2004).

Retelling a narrative can be difficult for children with DLD, partly because of the expressive language skills required to describe the people, places and events, all of which are essential elements. In addition, you need to sequence ideas and express linguistic concepts such as: now, first, next, last, before and after, all of which are challenging for children with DLD.

Phonological awareness

Phonological awareness is the ability to hear and manipulate the sounds in words at the level of syllables, rhymes and sounds. Knowing that 'cat' rhymes with 'hat' or has a 'c' sound at the beginning are both examples of phonological awareness. It is fundamental for learning new words, for speech sound development and for reading.

Children with DLD often need longer to develop their phonological awareness skills, which can impact on their developing literacy skills. Some children with DLD also have co-occurring difficulties with speech sound development, for example, saying 'dun' for sun or 'rai' for 'rain'. However, not all children with DLD have speech sound difficulties.

NOTE: many young children experience a specific difficulty developing their speech sounds, but they do not have any additional language needs. These children would not be classed as having DLD.

Why is language so important?

Language is central to all of our lives. We use language every day for building relationships, for working and learning, and for sharing our experiences and ideas.

Learning language is one of the most difficult things we learn to do, yet the majority of children will have grasped this skill quite naturally, before they even start school.

Learning language doesn't happen as fluently for children with DLD.

As highlighted here, language involves many different skills and children with DLD experience difficulties with several of these. A child's language needs are likely to vary at different times during their development, influenced by the social and academic demands at the time. As DLD affects each child slightly differently, you will need to talk to your child's speech and language therapist to find out what your child's individual strengths and needs are in terms of language.

2. What does *Harry's Story* teach us?

This chapter explores the impact of DLD, using examples from the picture book *Harry's Story*, along with strategies to support the child.

Difficulties understanding language

When a child doesn't understand language, they may be described as having receptive language difficulties. They can hear what people are saying but do not understand what all the words mean. Many children with DLD have receptive language difficulties which impacts on their understanding of sentences, instructions, questions and jokes.

Why does it happen?

If someone uses too many unfamiliar words, it is harder to understand the full meaning of what they are saying. This can happen to all of us sometimes. For example, if someone is using words that are specific to their job or interest, and we don't know much about it ourselves, we might not understand what they mean. We may even stop listening.

Children with DLD may be good at picking out familiar words, but they may struggle to understand the overall meaning. This means they may respond incorrectly or give an answer that seems over literal, or unrelated.

What does this look like for a child with DLD?

- They might appear to have poor attention and seem distracted.
- They might fidget when they are asked to listen to a story or follow instructions.
- They might look as if they are not listening.
- They might respond to the key words they understand, e.g., if you ask them 'point to the big dinosaur with the long neck' they might point to all the dinosaurs on the page.
- They might give a vague response or repeat some of the words you say, e.g., if you ask Where did you go on holiday? They might say 'go on holiday'.
- They might respond literally, e.g., if you ask them to throw out the milk. They might throw the milk.

DOI: 10.4324/9781003251965-4

Examples from *Harry's Story*

Harry doesn't know what he should be doing in class. He hasn't understood the instructions that his teacher has given. She may be using too many difficult words or giving a long sequence of instructions that Harry can't understand or remember.

Strategies: how to support children's understanding

- Give the child time to process what you have said. It might take them up to ten seconds so be patient.
- Check the child has understood the first part of an instruction before giving the next part.
- Keep your sentences and instructions short and simple.
  - Instead of: 'We're going to do some reading now for ten minutes, then after that we can go outside to play.'
  - Try: 'Reading now then play time.'
- Give a positive instruction and say what you want the child to do. They may have difficulty understanding negatives so might respond only to the key word that they understand.
  - Instead of: 'Don't run to class.'
  - Try: 'Let's walk to class.'

- Break long sentences and instructions into small steps.
  - Instead of: 'Put away your pencils and books in the blue tray at the back of the class then come and line up by door.'
  - Try: 'Put your pencil and book away' (wait for them to complete) 'Now line up by the door.'
- Give instructions in the order they need to be completed.
  - Instead of: 'Put your name on the board *after* you hang your coat up.'
  - Try: 'Hang your coat up *then* put your name on the board.'
- Using visual supports such as picture symbols, visual timetables and key word signing, alongside spoken language, can really support a child's understanding.
- Give the child a visual tabletop prompt to help them remember, sequence and plan tasks. This could be a step-by-step template of the task or a whiteboard with the key steps drawn or written on it. This can help children access lessons more independently.

Vocabulary and word finding difficulties

Difficulties with vocabulary are a common characteristic of DLD (Bishop et al 2017) and both receptive and expressive vocabulary may be affected. Word finding difficulties refer to that tip of the tongue feeling when you know a word in your head, but you just can't quite reach it to say it out loud. For some children with DLD this can happen frequently, and it disrupts the flow of their talking or means they lose their turn in the conversation.

Why does it happen?
When we learn a new word, it gets stored in our 'lexicon' (which is like our internal dictionary). Words are stored according to both their meaning and the sounds in the word. For children with DLD, words might be stored in a 'fuzzy' or more fragile way because of their wider language difficulties. They may have an idea of the word in their head but accessing the details of the word to say it out loud is difficult. This affects learning new words and means that children with DLD have a smaller vocabulary to choose from, which impacts on what they can tell you.

What does this look like for a child with DLD?
- They might hesitate and appear to have the word on the tip of their tongue.
- They might say another word that is similar in meaning or sound e.g., 'pushchair' instead of wheelchair.
- They might try to tell you something about the word, e.g., 'oh it's a . . . you wear it . . . it's a . . .''
- They might use non-specific words such as 'there', 'thingy', 'that' or 'it', rather than naming the word.

Examples from *Harry's Story*

Harry can't think of the right word for butterfly. He knows parts of this long word, but he is struggling to remember and organise them in the right way.

Harry is trying to say the word crocodile, but he says 'snap-snap-dile'. He knows that crocodiles go 'snap-snap' and he has inserted this into his version of the word. The word he has produced is related to the overall meaning of the word and it also has a similar sounding ending, 'dile'.

casst man

Tin man

man

Harry's word finding difficulties also appear in his writing. He is trying to think of the word 'knight' for his story, but it is a difficult word. It is not a word that is used in everyday conversation, and it also has an irregular spelling.

How to support word finding difficulties and vocabulary

- Ask the child if they want more time to think of the word themselves, or if they would like some help.
- Ask the child to tell you something about the meaning of the word. For example, 'Where do you see it?' or 'What does it look like?'
- Ask about the sound of the word 'What sound does it start with?' or 'Does it sound like another word?'
- Ask the child to show you a sign or an action to help you guess the word.
- It helps to pre-teach vocabulary, so the child is ready for learning and prepared for the lesson. If your child is learning about the Ancient Egyptians, give them the topic vocabulary in advance, then play some vocabulary games to learn and practise these words.

There are several published programmes and packages targeting vocabulary teaching. Ask your speech and language therapist or SENCO about these.

Difficulties with behaviour and social interactions

Some children with DLD may need support to join in social situations and to regulate their emotions and behaviours. This is because language plays an essential part in helping us to manage our thoughts, feelings and behaviours (Norbury, 2013). If children can't manage this verbally, then they are more likely to communicate through their behaviours. Increasing evidence highlights the links between language and behaviour and many children with DLD are likely to experience difficulties with social participation or regulating their behaviour at some point in their lives (RCSLT, 2018).

Why does it happen?

When children don't understand what is expected of them, they are more likely to get things wrong and potentially get into trouble. We know that children with DLD have difficulty understanding language which puts them at greater risk of making mistakes or misunderstanding situations.

In addition, children with DLD may struggle to use verbal reasoning, negotiating and narrative skills to explain what has happened, or why they behaved in a certain way.

What does this look like for a child with DLD?

- They might appear to be disobedient or uncooperative when really, they have not understood the instruction.
- They might get cross or frustrated if they don't understand what to do. Other children, however, might withdraw or become very quiet when a negative situation arises.
- They might struggle to tell you what happened, and it may be difficult for them to explain their side of the story.
- They might take something from a friend without asking, such as a toy or a game. Most children use language to ask and negotiate with sharing and turn taking but this is harder for children with DLD.
- They might need help joining in with other children's games. It is harder to join in and keep up with games and social situations when you have language difficulties.

Examples from *Harry's Story*

Harry's teacher looks cross that Harry is drawing when it is time to write. Harry looks worried and then embarrassed; he didn't understand the writing task and he didn't realise he had done something wrong. On top of this, Harry doesn't have the language skills to explain why writing is difficult for him or how drawing helps him.

Harry's language difficulties impact on his ability to join in with other children's games in the playground. Children's games often have complicated rules or narratives which can be difficult for children with DLD to keep up with and understand. Children don't always understand each other's differences, like the girls here who are giggling. They probably don't mean to be unkind, but their behaviour might make Harry feel sad.

How to support behaviour and social interactions

- One of the first and most important things is to stop and think 'what is causing this behaviour?' Thinking about why a child might be behaving in a certain way can be an important first step in identifying a potentially hidden language difficulty.

- Reduce your language and provide clear, consistent instructions. Check the child has understood the first step before giving the next part of the instruction. You might also need to use visual supports with some children (see the communication-friendly environments section, for more information).

- Teach your child social skills through small-group work. For example, use role play to practice asking how to join in a playground game.
- Teach your child how to ask for help. You may need to role play this together, e.g., practice phrases such as, 'Can you say it again' or 'I don't understand'. (See the activities section for further ideas.)
- For published resources to support and develop children's language for thinking and behaviour, see Parsons and Branagan (2017) and for slightly older children, see Branagan, Cross, and Parsons (2020).

Literacy difficulties

Literacy difficulties are challenges related to reading, spelling and written language. Literacy difficulties can affect reading and understanding words at single word and sentence level. Success with reading, and understanding what you have read, relies on decoding, remembering and understanding the meaning of words and sentences within a text. Success with writing relies on being able to fluently write words, sentences and texts that contain accurate spelling and grammar.

Why does it happen?

Children draw upon their spoken language skills to support their literacy development, so if a child has difficulties with spoken language, it is likely that they will also need help with written language. In essence, spoken language provides a foundation for literacy development and plays an important role in learning to read and write (Cain, 2010).

For some children with DLD, the increased language demands of learning to read and write highlight their spoken language difficulties, which may or may not have been previously identified (Bishop & Clarkson, 2003). Furthermore, the language used in written texts is often more descriptive and abstract than spoken language, which presents an additional challenge for children with DLD and impacts on their reading comprehension. Many children with DLD will therefore need support with reading and spelling, as well as understanding the meaning of written text.

What does this look like for a child with DLD?

- They might need more support learning their letters and sounds compared to their peers.
- They may be slower to develop their early phonics knowledge.
- They might prefer talking more generally about the pictures in their reading books, rather than reading the words.
- They might have difficulty understanding the meaning of words and sentences.
- They might need help with writing words and arranging them into sentences because of their associated language difficulties. We can't expect a child to write what they can't yet say in their own spoken language.
- It might take them longer to decode words and access their meanings. This means that they might forget what they have just read, which in turn affects the flow and the overall meaning of a text.

- Reading might not be enjoyable for all children with DLD, but for some, the permanence of written words compared to spoken language can be an advantage. Some children will benefit from being able to read and re-read a sentence to help them work out the meaning.

Examples from Harry's story

Harry is an imaginative boy with plenty of ideas for a story, but his language difficulties get in the way of expressing them. If Harry can't write his story down like everyone else in the class, he is at risk of not being able to share his ideas or show his creativity. Figures 2.8 and 2.9 show the contrast between what is going on in Harry's head, which is full of images, and what he can express in writing, which is completely blank.

How to support literacy difficulties
Reading

- It is really important to make book sharing an enjoyable and positive experience for children with DLD. Even if some of the words are difficult, the pictures can be a great support, so use them as much as your child needs. If your child wants to talk about the pictures, that's fine. You can use this time to introduce new vocabulary, talk about what's happening in the picture and talk about how the characters might be feeling. Pictures can also provide prompts to talk about our own experiences too.
- Allow your child to choose books that they are interested in, even if you have read them hundreds of times. Children with DLD need lots of repetition to learn language and will take comfort from the familiar language of a well-loved book.
- Point to the words as you read them aloud, this will help your child notice the link between the spoken and written words. Try not to put pressure on them if they're not ready to read aloud themselves.
- Read books that have rhymes or repeated refrains and encourage your child to join in with saying them aloud. This can help them learn the sound, rhyme and rhythm of words, which links to the development of phonological awareness.
- Talk to your child's teacher about their reading level and find out how you can help them at home.

Writing

- If your child enjoys drawing, encourage them to draw their ideas down on paper. Drawing helps children learn that their marks have meaning which is an important step in mark making and writing development.

- When your child is drawing you can add some language. You could talk about what the characters are doing in the picture, comment about the colours of their clothes/their hair, etc. This builds on the child's strengths rather than highlighting what is difficult. You are also giving the child valuable opportunities to practice spoken language structures, which means you are also putting in place the groundwork for their writing.

- Try to keep the mechanics of writing and spelling separate to the times you want your child's ideas to flow. If your child is stuck on spelling a word, they are likely to forget the rest of their sentence or story.

- Use a story planner to help your child think of the essential elements of the story. They could draw, or cut and stick pictures, to support their story planning. Then they can use this to support their writing.

- Allow your child plenty of time to carry out written tasks. If they can't finish anything they may feel as if they are failing, but this doesn't need to be the case.

Communication-friendly environment

As well as learning from Harry, we can also learn from his teacher, Miss Heart. She learns to listen to Harry and as a result, she begins to recognise his needs. By the end of the story, Miss Heart has made her classroom a little more communication friendly and she gives Harry extra support to help him with his learning.

Communication-friendly environments support and promote opportunities for meaningful interactions. They benefit all children, but they can be particularly supportive for children with communication difficulties (Dockrell et al, Ricketts et al, & Lindsay et al, 2012).

Whilst this term is often applied to schools and Early Years settings, the principles of a communication-friendly environment can also be applied to support families at home. Creating an environment that supports communication involves making some changes to the physical environment, as well as adults adapting their communication to match the needs of the child.

How do communication-friendly environments support children with DLD?

- Communication-friendly environments prompt adults to focus on what they can do better to support the child's needs, rather than just focusing on what the child finds difficult. This can be powerful because it shifts the idea of the 'problem' away from the child.

- When we adapt our environment and communicate in a more supportive way, we reduce the language demands on the child which in turn lessens the impact of their DLD.

- Changing the communication environment can have a positive impact for the child; allowing them to build relationships and increase their confidence in communicating.

Examples from *Harry's Story*

When Miss Heart comes down to Harry's level her body language becomes less intimidating, and she appears more interested in Harry's work. It will also be easier for Harry to communicate with her now because he can see her face and hear her words more easily.

How to create a communication-friendly environment

- Create a space that uses visual methods of communication to support understanding and use of language. This might include key word signing, photos and picture symbols.
- Create opportunities for language through 1:1 and small group activities, adult supported play and shared book reading.
- Make time to communicate with your child. Remember that children with DLD will need more time to process and use language, so be patient.
- Create positive interactions with your child by monitoring your language to support them. Think about:
  - Physically getting down to your child's level
  - Simplifying your language to match your child's language level
  - Giving your child time to process instructions
  - Waiting for them to respond
  - Not interrupting or answering for your child

- - Using comments rather than too many questions
  - Using gestures or key signs to support your spoken language
  - Keeping your language simple, e.g., jumper instead of 'pullover'.
- Speak to your speech and language therapist for further advice to help you make your home or learning environment more communication friendly.

3. Sharing *Harry's Story* with your child

This chapter aims to provide practical advice to help you talk to your child about DLD. There is information about developing the skills to be a supportive communication partner, as well as sample prompts and questions you can use when reading *Harry's Story* with your child.

The follow up activities aim to help you and your child:

- Talk about their strengths and their needs
- Identify what helps them
- Develop strategies and confidence to ask for help

Talking to children about DLD

Talking about DLD can be helpful for some children. It might explain why they find certain things at home or at school more difficult than other children.

Other children might not want to talk about what they find hard, or they may not be aware of their own difficulties with language yet.

It is important to respect your child's level of self-awareness and follow their lead in these conversations. When they are ready, talking about DLD with your child can be a positive step towards self-advocacy.

Self-advocacy is a practical strategy for all children to learn, especially children who are more likely to need extra help and support. Research suggests that promoting self-advocacy can be successful for children with learning needs, to help them develop self-confidence and independence to ask for the support they need (Pocock et al., 2002). Self-advocacy involves recognising and understanding your strengths and weaknesses, then identifying and talking about what helps you. It encourages children to say what they want and need help with, enabling them to be more involved in decisions about the support they receive.

Children with DLD will benefit from:

- A patient and supportive communication partner
- Opportunities for role play to develop confidence when asking for help
- Opportunities to talk with different people to show that everyone likes and needs help with different things

DOI: 10.4324/9781003251965-5

Involving children in decision making

The SEND Code of Practice (Department for Education, 2015) recognises that all children with special educational needs should be asked about their feelings and wishes and consulted about the support that is put in place for them. Whilst this is a positive approach, it presents a challenge for children with language and communication needs (Bloom et al., 2020) because talking about thoughts, feelings and future hopes involves several different language skills.

Look at the following examples. Consider whether your child could understand and use this language.

- Understanding 'how', 'why' and 'what if' questions.
    - 'How could you change your school to make it better for you?'
    - What would school look like if you could change three things?'
- Using complex sentences and verbal reasoning to give explanations, express thoughts and ideas and to make predictions.
    - 'I would . . .'
    - 'It would be better if . . .'
- Understanding and using mental state verbs (e.g., think, believe, know, wish) to talk about feelings and wishes.
    - 'I think I am good at maths and football'.
    - 'I wish I didn't have to be on my own at lunch time.'

Parents, teachers and professionals will need to be mindful of the child's language needs and provide appropriate support when talking about strengths and needs. It might take practice to follow and support the conversations of children with language difficulties, but with a little patience you can make a positive difference.

Top tips for talking to children with DLD

Find a quiet space
When it is noisy, it can be difficult for children with DLD to tune out the background noise and tune in to language. Find a quiet space to help them focus better and join in the conversation.

Remove distractions
Help your child focus on conversations by removing any toys or objects that might distract them.

Remember to remove your own distractions too so you can give your full attention to your child; turn off your phone, computer, emails, radio or TV.

Know how the child communicates

If you are not the child's parent, make sure you know them well and how they communicate. For example, if you know the child likes to use picture symbols or photographs to help them communicate make sure these are available for them to use. You will both get a lot more out of the conversation if the child trusts you and feels relaxed talking to you.

Take time

Be patient and give your child plenty of time to think and respond. It often takes children with DLD longer to understand and respond to what has been said, so it's important they don't feel rushed. Slowing down your own talking, and taking time to pause in conversation, can make a positive difference.

Use simple language

Children with DLD often struggle with grammar and complicated sentence structures. It is important to simplify your own language to help your child understand what you are saying. Try to use words that the child is familiar with and keep your sentences short and simple.

Reduce questions

Too many questions can be difficult for children with DLD, especially 'why' and 'how' questions. We will talk more about questions later in this chapter, but they key message for now is to avoid asking too many questions, especially ones where you already know the answer.

Listen

Listen to what the child is telling you and try hard not to interrupt or ask leading questions. You could occasionally repeat what the child has said, to show them you have listened and understood.

Take breaks

Give your child time to take a break if they need it or aim to keep sessions as short as they need. You might want to do a few sessions to read *Harry's Story* and talk about it with your child.

Talking about feelings, thoughts and wishes

We use specific words to talk about our feelings, thoughts and emotions and children with DLD may need extra support to use these words, just as they would for any other new vocabulary.

Emotion words

Emotion words are describing words to explain how people feel. They include sad, angry, happy, scared, worried, excited.

Children with DLD might know more familiar emotion words like happy, sad and angry but struggle with less frequently used words such as embarrassed, worried, or confused. They may also find it hard if there are lots of different words that mean a similar thing, e.g., scared, worried, fearful, frightened.

You can support children to learn and use emotion words by:

- Talking about what someone looks like when they feel an emotion, e.g., the boy is smiling because he is happy.
- Giving examples of situations that might make someone feel that emotion, e.g., the boy is happy because it's his birthday.
- Linking these emotion words to our own experiences, which adds context and meaning.

Examples:

- Embarrassed
  - 'Embarrassed is feeling like I've done something silly. My face turns red when I'm embarrassed. I feel embarrassed when I fall over in front of everyone.'
- Happy
  - 'Happy is feeling like everything is good. I smile and laugh when I am happy. I feel happy when I go to the beach.'

Mental state verbs

We use mental state verbs to express what we are doing in our mind. They include words like thinking, believing, remembering, knowing, wondering and wishing.

We use mental state verbs to talk about our feelings and wishes, which are important in decision making. Mental state verbs are harder for children to learn because they don't label something that can be seen or touched. It's not easy to see the action of wishing or feeling for example.

You can begin to help children understand and use these words by:

- Talking about these words when you are sharing books. In *Harry's Story* for example, you could say:
  - 'Harry is **thinking** of ideas for his story.'
  - 'Harry can't **remember** the word for butterfly.'
  - 'Miss Heart **knows** the pictures help Harry.'
- Supporting what you say with body language and facial expressions that are associated with these words, e.g., looking confused if you can't remember.

Comments, prompts and questions?

Sometimes it feels as if the only way to find something out is to ask lots of questions but when we take time to watch and listen, we can find out even more.

Look at the following examples to see how questions impact on our interactions:

Example 1

Adult: Harry looks happy here. What makes you happy?

Child: No response.

Adult: What do you like doing?

Child: Swimming.

Adult: Why do you like swimming?

Child: No response (child looks confused?)

Adult: Where do you go swimming?

Child: I go swimming with Mummy.

Adult: Oh lovely. Does Mummy like swimming?

Example 2

Adult: Look Harry is happy (pause and wait)

Child: Him jump. (points)

Adult: That's right he's happy and he's jumping. I like singing when I'm happy. (pause and wait)

Child: I do singing.

Adult: Wow, you like singing too. What else do you like? (use gesture to support)

Child: I like singing and football and cooking and football.

Adult: Lucky you. Lots of things make you happy.

In Example 1, the adult uses a lot of questions which makes the conversation feel one sided. It's more difficult for the child to understand and answer all these questions.

In Example 2, the adult uses more comments. This makes the conversation feel more balanced and the adult learns more, even though they only asked one question.

Why are questions difficult for children with DLD?

When we ask a question, it demands an answer. This can be a challenge for children with DLD because:

- They might not understand question words, especially 'why?' and 'how?'
- They might not have the expressive language skills to give the expected answer.

- They might feel under pressure to respond, which could impact on their language skills and ability to answer.

Blank, Rose, and Berlin (1978) developed a framework to show the development of question words, which can help us identify which questions are more difficult for children to understand. The framework is referred to as 'Blank Levels' and there are four levels of questions, which are briefly outlined here:

Blank Level 1: Naming	What is that? What is the boy doing?
Blank Level 2: Describing	Where is the cat hiding? What else can you drive? Who else is running?
Blank Level 3: Re-telling	What happened to the boy? What did you do at lunch time? What will happen next?
Blank Level 4: Justifying and reasoning	Why did you throw the ball? How does the girl feel? What would you do if you fell over?

Blank Levels 1 and 2 are the most concrete and generally refer to what the child can see in front of them. They link to what is happening here and now.

Blank Levels 3 and 4 are less concrete and require the child to be able to talk about the past, sequence events, justify actions and make predictions.

Keeping the 'Blank Levels' in mind can be a good strategy to help us to keep our language at the right level for our child. It also reminds us why our child can't always respond to questions in the way we expect.

If you notice that your child is struggling to answer a Blank Level 4 question, try simplifying your language and asking a Blank Level 3 question.

Adult: Why is Billy crying?
Child: Billy crying.
Adult: What happened at play time?
Child: I throwed a ball on Billy.

If your child doesn't understand a question, you can model an answer to help them.

Adult: How is Billy feeling?

Child: No response (points to Billy)

Adult: Billy feels sad. He is crying.

Remember that comments can be powerful too. With a little support and patience, your child may tell you what you want to know, without so many questions.

Aim to use more comments than questions in conversation, ideally one question to every four comments.

If you're not sure what questions your child understands, or if you want to find out more about Blank Levels, you could talk to your child's speech and language therapist or speak to the SENCO at your child's school.

Sample prompts and questions to use alongside *Harry's Story*

This section provides prompts, along with questions, that you could use whilst you are reading *Harry's Story* with your child.

There are simple questions, which are associated with Blank Levels 1 and 2 and extension questions, which are associated with Blank Levels 3 and 4.

Top tips for using prompts and questions:

- Use the prompts and questions as a guide rather than asking your child every one.
- Aim to keep a natural, conversational style when you are book-sharing.
- Point to the part of the picture you are talking about.
- Use a combination of prompts and questions.
- If your child can't answer the extension questions, try asking the simple questions.
- Listen to and acknowledge your child's responses.
- Prompt for more information
  - 'What else . . . ?'/'Can you tell me more?'
- Show you have understood by modelling back and adding to what your child has said.
  - 'That's right Harry doesn't know what to do. I feel worried when I don't know what to do.'
- Provide model answers if your child can't answer easily.
  - 'Why does Harry look confused? . . . Harry looks confused **because** he doesn't know how to play the game.'
- Use Harry's character as an example then ask about the child's experience.
  - 'Has this ever happened to you?'

Page 1–2	
 Harry is a little boy with a wide and happy smile.	But sounds and words are difficult, so talking takes a while. 
Prompts	Harry looks happy. Harry has a lovely big smile. Harry looks confused here. Harry's thinking 'butterwings, flutterby'. Harry can't think of the word for butterfly. Talking is hard for Harry. Harry has Developmental Language Disorder/DLD.
Simple Questions	Can you make a big smile like Harry? What is this called? (point to butterfly) Can you think of something else that flies?
Extension Questions	Why does Harry look confused? What words are difficult for you to remember? What words are difficult for you to say? What is Harry thinking?

Page 3–4

At school he likes his teacher and his friends are really kind.

But words are hard to understand and words are hard to find.

Prompts	Harry looks happy here. Harry doesn't know what game the girls are playing. Harry doesn't know the word for crocodile. He is saying snap-snap-dile. The girls are laughing at Harry.
Simple Questions	Where is Harry's teacher? What game are the girls playing? What is Harry doing here? (point to his 'crocodile' arms)
Extension Questions	What games do you like playing at school? Who do you like playing with at school? Why do you think the girls are laughing? How is Harry feeling here? What makes you feel happy/sad?

Page 5–6

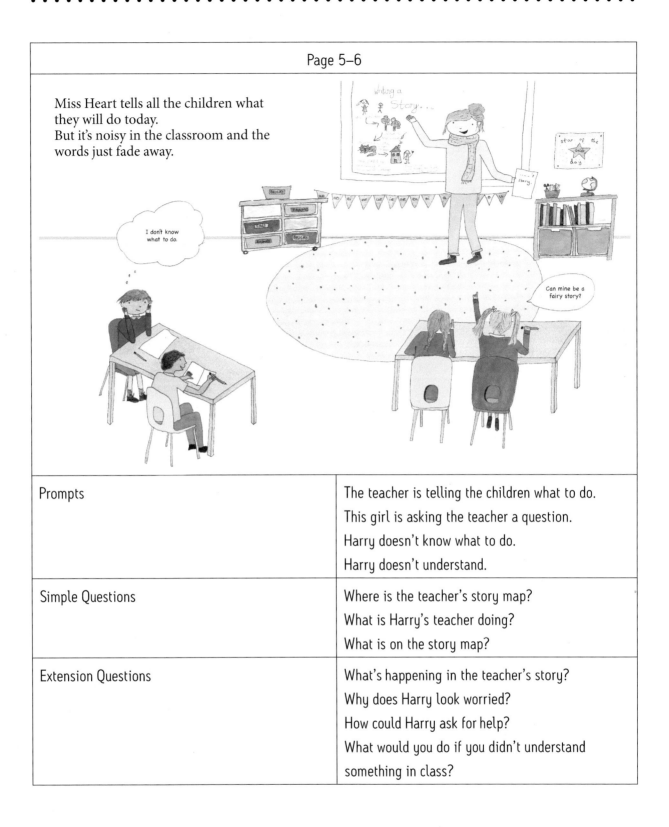

Miss Heart tells all the children what they will do today.
But it's noisy in the classroom and the words just fade away.

Prompts	The teacher is telling the children what to do. This girl is asking the teacher a question. Harry doesn't know what to do. Harry doesn't understand.
Simple Questions	Where is the teacher's story map? What is Harry's teacher doing? What is on the story map?
Extension Questions	What's happening in the teacher's story? Why does Harry look worried? How could Harry ask for help? What would you do if you didn't understand something in class?

Pages 7–8

Prompts	This little girl knows what to do. This is what Harry is thinking about. Harry has got lots of good ideas. I can see a scary dragon. Harry is thinking about a castle and a king.
Simple Questions	Who is this? (point to the king/dragon) What is this boy doing? (point to boy who is writing) What can you see here? (point to thought bubble)
Extension Questions	What could Harry write about? Why isn't Harry writing yet?

Page 9–10	
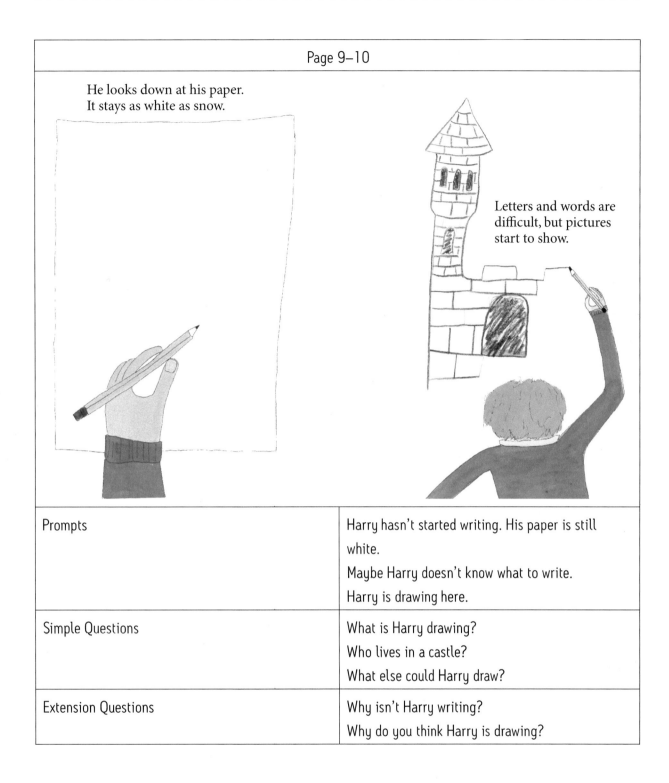 He looks down at his paper. It stays as white as snow.	Letters and words are difficult, but pictures start to show.
Prompts	Harry hasn't started writing. His paper is still white. Maybe Harry doesn't know what to write. Harry is drawing here.
Simple Questions	What is Harry drawing? Who lives in a castle? What else could Harry draw?
Extension Questions	Why isn't Harry writing? Why do you think Harry is drawing?

Pages 11–12	
He starts at the beginning, with a brave and shining knight. ~~Casst Man~~ ~~Fin Man~~ ~~Man~~ He can't think of the word for knight….	But he can draw one, just right.

Prompts	Look at Harry's writing. He can't think of the word to write. Harry has drawn a knight. A knight is a soldier for the king or queen. Harry's drawing is helping him.
Simple Questions	What is the knight holding? Who else lives in a castle?
Extension Questions	What do you like about Harry's drawing? What helps you in class? Who do you ask when you need help at school?

Pages 13–14

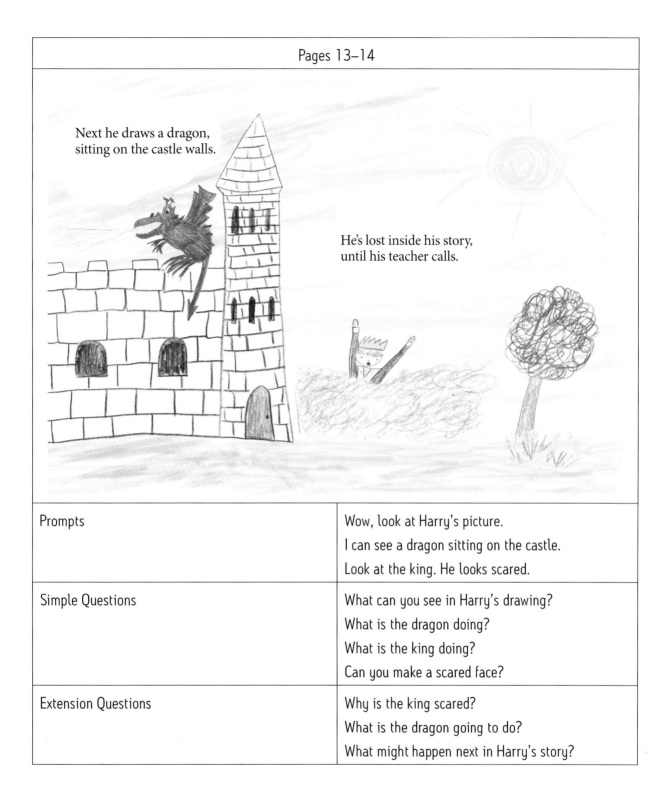

Next he draws a dragon, sitting on the castle walls.

He's lost inside his story, until his teacher calls.

Prompts	Wow, look at Harry's picture. I can see a dragon sitting on the castle. Look at the king. He looks scared.
Simple Questions	What can you see in Harry's drawing? What is the dragon doing? What is the king doing? Can you make a scared face?
Extension Questions	Why is the king scared? What is the dragon going to do? What might happen next in Harry's story?

Pages 15–16

"What are you doing Harry? It's not the time to draw."

Harry feels embarrassed. He looks down at the floor.

Prompts	Oh dear, Harry's teacher looks cross. Harry looks worried. Harry looks embarrassed. Poor Harry, he didn't want to upset his teacher. (point to the question marks) Harry doesn't know why his teacher is cross.
Simple Questions	Can you make a cross face? Can you make a worried face? Can you make an embarrassed face?
Extension Questions	Why is the teacher cross with Harry? Why does Harry look worried? How do we know Harry is embarrassed? What might happen next?

Pages 17–18	
"My story got a dragon." Harry tells Miss Heart.	"That one got some fire in him." And he pointed to his art.

Prompts	Harry is showing his teacher his drawings. Well done Harry. Harry looks happy talking to his teacher. Harry is showing Miss Heart that his pictures make a story.
Simple Questions	What is Harry doing here? What is Harry pointing to?
Extension Questions	How does Harry feel now? What will Harry's teacher say?

Pages 19–20	
Miss Heart looked at his drawings …  … and she saw the story flow. 	She thought …. "Those pictures help Harry. I'm so glad that I know." 
Prompts	Harry's ideas go together to make a story. Look at the dragon breathing out fire. The birthday cake looks delicious. Miss Heart knows Harry likes drawing. Harry's teacher looks happy here.
Simple Questions	What is the dragon/king/knight doing? (point to one of Harry's drawings) Where is the birthday cake? Do you like drawing? How many drawings are there?
Extension Questions	Tell me about the drawing you like best? What do you think happens in Harry's story? What would help you in class? How does Harry's teacher feel now? Why is Harry's teacher happy now?

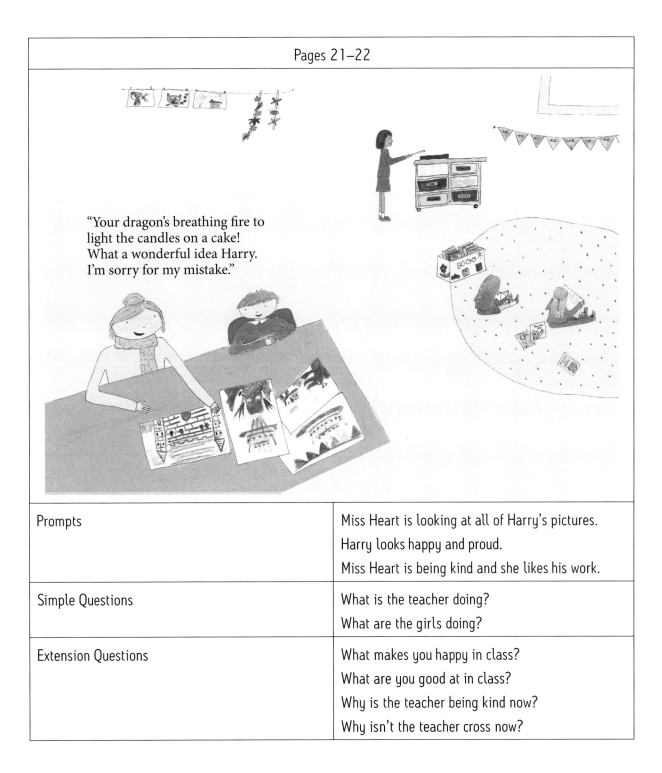

Pages 21–22	
Prompts	Miss Heart is looking at all of Harry's pictures. Harry looks happy and proud. Miss Heart is being kind and she likes his work.
Simple Questions	What is the teacher doing? What are the girls doing?
Extension Questions	What makes you happy in class? What are you good at in class? Why is the teacher being kind now? Why isn't the teacher cross now?

"Your dragon's breathing fire to light the candles on a cake! What a wonderful idea Harry. I'm sorry for my mistake."

Pages 23–24	

Prompts	Miss Heart has given the children pencils and paints. Some of the other children like drawing pictures too.
Simple Questions	What are the children drawing? What is Harry drawing? Who else is drawing?
Extension Questions	How does Harry feel now? What do you like in Harry's classroom? What would make your classroom better for learning? What do you like about Harry's teacher? What helps you with writing in class?

Text on illustration: So Miss Heart changed her classroom. There's pictures, paints and glue. Now Harry smiles at story time and he knows just what to do.

Follow up activities

COMPANION @ WEBSITE

1. Children's profiles

More children have DLD than you might think. Around two children in every class.

All of these children have DLD. Find out what they like, what they find hard and what helps them.

Bella

AGE: 7
LIKES: Mountain biking and baking.
WHAT'S HARD AT SCHOOL?
Remembering and saying sentences.
Saying the right sounds in words.
Reading.
WHAT HELPS? When people give me
time to talk. Playing games to practice
speech sounds. Talking about simple
stories with pictures.

Arlo

AGE: 8
LIKES: Science and skateboarding
WHAT'S HARD AT SCHOOL: Using new
words in sentences. Remembering long
words.
WHAT HELPS: Pre-teaching vocabulary
especially science words. Giving me
time to say what I want to say.

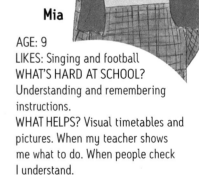

Mia

AGE: 9
LIKES: Singing and football
WHAT'S HARD AT SCHOOL?
Understanding and remembering
instructions.
WHAT HELPS? Visual timetables and
pictures. When my teacher shows
me what to do. When people check
I understand.

Lani

AGE: 11
LIKES: Singing and playing on
the computer
WHAT'S HARD AT SCHOOL:
Joining in conversations.
Organising and writing my work
in class.
WHAT HELPS: Narrative group
games. Using a story planner.
Planning my ideas on comic
strips.

Eddie

AGE: 10
LIKES: Superhero comics and
swimming
WHAT'S HARD AT SCHOOL?
Understanding jokes. Making friends.
Joining in playground games.
WHAT HELPS? When adults teach and
practice jokes with me. Knowing I can
ask adults for help.

Jackson

AGE: 5
LIKES: Drawing and Lego
WHAT'S HARD AT SCHOOL: Writing.
Learning and remembering new words.
WHAT HELPS? Drawing my ideas.
Extra time to learn new words. Using
pictures and photos to help me.

2. What about you?

Name: ....

> Draw yourself
> or
> stick a photo here

AGE:

LIKES:

WHAT'S HARD AT SCHOOL: .

WHAT HELPS:

3. Easy or hard?

In the story Harry finds some things hard, like understanding instructions and writing.

Other things are easy for him, like drawing and thinking of ideas for stories.

Talk to a friend or a grown-up about what is easy and hard for you. You can use the cards provided here or think of your own ideas.

Talking with my friends	Art and craft	Joining in with playground games
Understanding instructions	Drawing pictures	Putting ideas in the right order
Building and making things	Writing stories	Saying the right words
Understanding jokes	Spelling	Asking my teacher for help
Thinking of stories	Explaining what happened	Learning new words
Playing sports	Playing music	Maths
Reading	Dancing	Working on a computer/tablet

Easy

Hard

4. How to ask for help

Do you know how to ask for help when you don't understand something?

Cut out these cards and talk about which ones are a good idea and which ones are not a good idea.

There are some blank cards to write down any good ideas of your own.

Hide under the table	Put my hand up and wait for help	Copy my friends
Do nothing	Ask my teacher to write or draw a checklist to help me complete the work	Ask my teacher to show me
Ask my teacher to say it again	Sit and stare out of the window	Shout until my teacher comes to help me
Get cross and shout at my teacher	Ask my friend to check I have understood	Walk out of the classroom

Good idea	Not good idea

5. Asking for help

At the beginning of the story Harry doesn't know what to do in class. He doesn't understand.

At the end of the story Harry talks to his teacher and shows her that drawing helps him in class.

It's good to talk to someone when you need help.

We all need help sometimes and different people need help with different things.

Some people need help with . . .

Seeing	Hearing
Remembering	Writing

Here are some more examples:

- 'Some people need help to see. They wear glasses to help them.'
- 'Some people need help with cooking. They use a recipe book to help them.'
- 'Some people need help with maths. They use a calculator to help them.'
- 'Some people need help with swimming. They use floats to help them.'

Activity 1

Ask a friend or grown-up what they need help with and who helps them.

Use these question cards to help if you need.

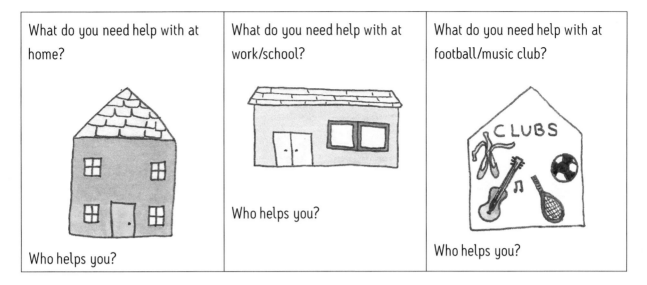

| What do you need help with at home? | What do you need help with at work/school? | What do you need help with at football/music club? |

Who helps you? (home)

Who helps you? (work/school)

Who helps you? (football/music club)

Activity 2

Use the cards below to practice asking for help with a friend or a grown-up. There are some blank cards so you can add your own ideas.

Take turns saying the phrases out loud. Then you will know what to say when you really need to ask for help.

Adults could:

• Give your child instructions to draw a pattern/a picture. Can they ask you to say it again when they don't understand?

• Read a page from a story out loud. Try reading it very fast. Can they ask you to slow down?

• Read a question from your maths book out loud. Can your child tell you if they don't understand a word?

| Can you say it again? | I don't understand. |

Say it again

?

COMPANION @ WEBSITE

Can you show me what to do?	Can you help me?

I don't know that word. What does it mean? 	Can you say it slowly? 
I can't remember what to do. Can you help me? 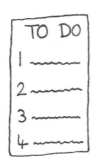	There are too many words I don't understand. 
Can I have more time? 	Can you write it down or draw it for me? 

References

Bishop, D. V. M., & Clarkson, B. (2003). Written language as a window into residual language deficits: A study of children with persistent and residual speech and language impairments. *Cortex, 39*(2): 215–237.

Bishop, D. V. M., Snowling, M. J., Thompson, P. A., & Greenhalgh, T. (2017). Phase 2 of CATALISE: A multinational and multidisciplinary Delphi consensus study of problems with language development: Terminology. *Journal of Child Psychology and Psychiatry, 58*: 1068–1080. https://doi.org/10.1111/jcpp.12721

Bishop, D. V. M., Snowling, M. J., Thompson, P. A., Greenhalgh, T., & The CATALISE Consortium. (2016). CATALISE: A multinational and multidisciplinary Delphi consensus study. Identifying language impairments in children. *PLoS One, 11*(7). http://dx.doi.org/10.1371/journal.pone.0158753

Blank, M., Rose, S. A., & Berlin, L. J. (1978). *The language of learning: The preschool years*. New York, NY: Grune & Stratton.

Bloom, A., Critten, S., Johnson, H., & Wood, C. (2020). Evaluating a method for eliciting children's voice about educational support with children with speech, language and communication needs. *British Journal of Special Education, 47*: 170–207. https://doi.org/10.1111/1467-8578.12308

Branagan, A., Cross, M., & Parsons, S. (2020). *Language for Behaviour and Emotions: A Practical Guide to Working with Children and Young People* (1st ed.). Abingdon, Oxon. Routledge.

Cain, K. (2010). *Reading development and difficulties: An introduction*. Oxford: BPS Textbooks in Psychology, Wiley-Blackwell.

Catts, H. W., Fey, M. E., Tomblin, J. B., & Zhang, X. (2002). A longitudinal investigation of reading outcomes in children with language impairments. *Journal of Speech, Language & Hearing Research, 45*(6): 1142–1157.

Department for Education and Department of Health. (2015). *Special educational needs and disability code of practice: 0 to 25 years*. Available at: www.gov.uk/government/publications/send-code-of-practice-0-to-25.

Dockrell, J., Ricketts, J. and Lindsay G., (2012). *Understanding Speech, Language and Communication Needs: Profiles of Need and Provision.* London: Department for Education (DfE). Available at: https://www.gov.uk/government/collection/better- communication-research-programme.

Griffin, T., Hemphill, L., Camp, L., & Wolf, D. (2004). Oral discourse in the preschool years and later literacy skills. *First Language, 24*: 123–147.

Lindsay, G., Dockrell, J., Law, J., & Roulstone, S. (2012). *The better communication research programme: Improving provision for children and young people with speech, language, and communication needs.* London: Department for Education (DfE). Available at: www.gov. uk/government/collection/better-communication-research- programme.

Muter, V., Hulme, C., Snowling, M. J., & Stevenson, J. (2004). Phonemes, rimes, vocabulary, and grammatical skills as foundations of early reading development: Evidence from a longitudinal study. *Developmental Psychology, 40*(5): 665–681.

Norbury, C. F. (2013). Editorial: Are you speaking my language? Raising awareness of language learning impairments in developmental psychopathology. *Journal of Child Psychology and Psychiatry, 54*: 705–706.

Norbury, C. F., Gooch, D., Wray, C., Baird, G., Charman, T., Simonoff, E., Vamvakas, G., & Pickles, A. (2016). The impact of nonverbal ability on prevalence and clinical presentation of language disorder: Evidence from a population study. *Journal of Child Psychology and Psychiatry, 57*(11): 1247–1257.

Parsons, S., & Branagan, A. (2017). *Language for thinking: A structured approach for young children.* Abingdon, Oxon: Routledge.

Pinto, G., Tarchi, C., & Bigozzi, L. (2015). The relationship between oral and written narratives: A three-year longitudinal study of narrative cohesion, coherence, and structure. *British Journal of Educational Psychology, 85*(4): 551–569.

Pocock, A., Lambros, S., Karvonen, M., et al. (2002). Successful strategies for promoting self-advocacy among students with LD: The LEAD group. *Intervention in School and Clinic, 37*(4): 209–216. doi:10.1177/105345120203700403

Royal Collage of Speech and Language Therapists. (2018). *Giving voice to people with language disorder.* Available at: www.rcslt.org/wp-content/uploads/media/Project/RCSLT/rcslt-dld-factsheet.pdf.

Additional reading and websites

Sowerbutts, A., & Finer, A. (2019). *DLD and me: Supporting children and young people with developmental language disorder.* Abingdon, Oxon: Routledge.

www.afasic.org.uk

www.dldandme.co.uk

www.ican.org.uk

www.naplic.org.uk

www.radld.org

Index